Essential Events

THE ASSASSINATION OF JOHN F. KENNEDY

THE ASSASSINATION OF
JOHN F. KENNEDY

BY PATRICIA M. STOCKLAND

Content Consultant
Sheldon M. Stern, Ph.D., Historian and Educational Consultant
Former Historian, John F. Kennedy Library
Boston, Massachusetts, 1976-1999

ABDO
Publishing Company

CREDITS

Published by ABDO Publishing Company, 8000 West 78th Street, Edina, Minnesota
55439. Copyright © 2008 by Abdo Consulting Group, Inc. International copyrights
reserved in all countries. No part of this book may be reproduced in any form without
written permission from the publisher. The Essential Library™ is a trademark and
logo of ABDO Publishing Company.

Printed in the United States.

Editor: Karen Latchana Kenney
Cover Design: Becky Daum
Interior Design: Lindaanne Donohoe

Library of Congress Cataloging-in-Publication Data
Stockland, Patricia M.
  The assassination of John F. Kennedy / Patricia M. Stockland.
      p. cm.—(Essential events)
  Includes bibliographical references and index.
  ISBN-13: 978-1-59928-848-2
  1. Kennedy, John F. (John Fitzgerald), 1917-1963—Assassination—Juvenile literature.
I. Title.
  E842.9.S73 2007
  973.922092—dc22

                                                          2007011999

TABLE OF CONTENTS

Lee Harvey Oswald holds his gun in a photo taken in his backyard.

BUYING A GUN

On January 28, 1963, a man by the alias "A.J. Hidell" placed a mail order. The purchase was a Smith & Wesson .38 special revolver from Seaport Traders. This shipment was to be delivered to Hidell's post office box in Dallas, Texas.

Six weeks later, on March 12, Hidell placed an order to Klein's Sporting Goods. This time, Hidell bought a 6.5 mm Mannlicher-Carcano Italian military rifle with a four-power scope.

Both guns arrived in Dallas on March 20. Hidell was excitedly awaiting their arrival. He was so proud of his guns that on March 31, he posed for photographs with them in his backyard. His Russian-born wife, Marina, took pictures of him dressed in black and holding his new firearms. She did not understand why her husband was so proud of the purchases. She was not comfortable having guns in their home and around their young daughter, June. Marina thought the request for the photos was strange, but she obediently stopped hanging laundry and took the pictures.

Later that week, Marina's husband developed the photos of himself at work. "He brought one back to [her] and inscribed on the back: 'For Junie from Papa.'"[1] Marina could not understand why her husband would give such a strange photograph to their daughter.

A Questionable Weapon

The Mannlicher-Carcano Italian rifle was not considered a reliable gun by some. Many European owners considered the firearm undependable and inaccurate. The FBI disagrees, noting the rifle does not have a hard kickback and is quite accurate.

Marina did not know that her husband had ordered the guns under a different name. Nor did she know what he planned to do with them. Her husband was a very secretive man with an explosive temper, and she was afraid to ask too many questions. She only knew her husband by his birth name, Lee Harvey Oswald.

Born October 18, 1939, the 24-year-old Oswald had spent his previous years in a variety of questionable situations. His childhood was far from idyllic and his marriage was also tumultuous. Oswald was raised by his widowed mother. She sent him to an orphanage, then a boarding school, and then back to an orphanage. During his school years, Lee spent many days skipping his classes. Instead, he rode around New York City's subway system and loitered in public places. Eventually he was caught, and the court sent him to a detention center. After a psychiatric evaluation that revealed him to be an emotionally neglected, closed-off—but not mentally disturbed—individual, Lee was released.

Soon after, he discovered the idea of socialism while reading some Russian spy literature. This discovery was an important one in shaping Oswald's adult path. At age 16, he joined the Civil Air Patrol, and at 17, the Marines. Within a short time, Oswald's marksmanship training earned him the title of "sharpshooter." By normal accuracy standards, he was an excellent shot. Oswald was stationed in Japan in 1957 and by 1958 was learning how to speak the Russian language. By 1959, he was making plans to defect to Russia and one year later had done so.

Oswald had an explosive temper and often found himself in trouble with higher-ranking officers. After defecting to Russia, where he met Marina, his temper did not lessen. Both the KGB and the CIA tracked him. Now, the couple had returned to the United States. Oswald's anger, military training, and loyalty to communism led to an animosity toward the United States and its leadership.

Over the next months of 1963, Oswald watched the newspapers. He closely followed politics and international events. He also kept secret diaries, notes, and plans. One plan Oswald had developed was an attack on General Edwin Walker. Walker was a right-wing activist in Texas who was getting a fair deal of publicity. He supported segregation. Oswald strongly believed in integrating people of all races and ethnicities.

June

Lee and Marina Oswald's daughter, June, was born while the couple was still living in Russia. After defecting to the Soviet Union, it took Oswald 18 months of persistent requests before authorities would let him reenter the United States with his new family.

Oswald's planned attack failed. He tried to take Walker's life on the night of April 10, but the single shot Oswald fired missed. He was not caught or even suspected of his attempted murder plot. And so, Oswald continued to watch the news and follow public events. He was particularly displeased with the U.S. treatment of Cuba and other communist nations. Oswald supported communism and considered himself a Marxist.

President Kennedy had been trying to slow the spread of communism. He was promoting democracy in less-developed nations and had allowed attacks on Cuba. The president had also stopped the Soviets from building nuclear launch sites in Cuba. None of this pleased Oswald.

Kennedy had a trip planned to Dallas in November. Oswald would attend and watch the presidential parade, like thousands of other Texans. But he had another plan in mind—a plan to show his dislike for the United States and its leadership.

Neither Marina nor the mail order companies suspected how Oswald's firearm purchases would change the course of history. By the end of that year, President John F. Kennedy would visit Dallas, Texas, for the last time—and meet an assassin's bullet.

Lee Harvey Oswald and his wife, Marina, pose on a bridge walk
in Minsk during their stay in the Soviet Union.

Young John F. Kennedy (seated), his brother and three sisters are shown in 1923 with their mother, Rose Kennedy.

THE KENNEDY HISTORY

In the mid-1800s, the United States experienced a swell of Irish immigrants. The year 1888 marked the birth of Joseph Patrick Kennedy, known by family and friends as "Joe." He was a descendent of this immigration boom and son of saloon owner P.J. Kennedy. The beginning of the Kennedy clan's life in politics can be traced back to P.J., who was considered a generous businessman in Boston's Second Ward. This positive image of generosity eventually led voters to elect P.J. to the state legislature. Later, he was appointed to the wire commissioner post for Boston.

P.J.'s son, Joe, learned both business and politics from his father's experience in the saloon and legislative sessions. With these skills, Joe would one day achieve financial success. In 1914, Joe married Rose Fitzgerald, whose father was also a politician. John F. Fitzgerald was known as "Honey Fitz" Fitzgerald for his smooth talk and always-ready answers. With a history of politics on both sides of the family, Joe and Rose's children were bound for civic duty at some point in their lives. Joe's intent was that, someday, one of his sons would be president of the United States.

"Honey Fitz" Fitzgerald

"Honey Fitz" Fitzgerald was John F. Kennedy's maternal grandfather. He served as Boston mayor from 1906 to 1907 and 1910 to 1914. He had previously served three terms in Congress, the first starting in 1894. Fitzgerald's smooth talking eventually became a point of amusement among voters. They referred to it as "Fitzblarney," meaning empty talk. But it was true that the politician did love to talk. According to a family friend, "Nothing made him happier than attending two or three functions in a single evening, and a Boston newspaper estimated that he had made 3,000 speeches in his first two years as mayor."[1]

Joe became a very successful businessman. As the Kennedy children came along, the family quickly moved from a middle-class lifestyle to living a life of financial luxury. Joe and Rose's second child, John Fitzgerald Kennedy, was born on May 29, 1917. Known as "Jack" to family and friends, he was often ill as a child. Illness did not affect his attitude, however. With plenty of time spent in bed, Jack read to entertain himself. He also made the most of every minute when he was well. Jack loved sports and sailing. In a family of nine children and numerous cousins, there were always plenty of people around to play a pickup game of football or swim races.

Although Jack's grades in school were only average,

The Kennedy Family's Rise to Wealth

John F. (Jack) Kennedy was the fourth generation of his family in the United States. His great-grandfather, Patrick Kennedy, had emigrated from Ireland during the potato famine. He died in 1858 and his widow, Bridget, raised Jack's grandfather, P.J. In 1888, Jack's father, Joe, was born and P.J. was already seeing success as a business owner and politician. Joe quickly caught on to making money and influencing people. Joe wanted to be rich and successful. He hoped to pave an easier life for his own children, wanting them, especially his sons, to achieve political greatness. It seems Jack's destiny was being built for him before he was even born. Indeed, by the time Jack was born, "Kennedy" was already a well-known name in the United States. By the time Jack ran for office, the Kennedy family was one of the wealthiest and most powerful in the nation.

his winning personality touched both teachers and fellow students. By the time he started college at Harvard, Jack was coming into his own as a smart person who was fun to be around. Jack had inherited his father's and grandfathers' industrious natures as well. He led many activities throughout college and was elected to various offices. He even traveled the world, despite still struggling with occasional bouts of illness.

The Battle for Good Health

Throughout his life, John F. Kennedy was plagued with a variety of illnesses. For most of his childhood, doctors were unable to diagnose the cause of his sickness. It was not until 1947 that Kennedy finally dis-covered he had Addison's disease. This disease causes back pain, vomiting, stomach pain, and diarrhea.

During his last year of college, Jack was able to travel for some time in Europe. His father was the U.S. ambassador to the court of St. James in England. At that time, the European continent was experiencing growing tension over German rearmament. The United States and England wanted to avoid involvement with these problems. But by the time Jack returned to the United States, World War II was unfolding. For his senior paper, he wrote his observations of why he believed England had tried to stay out of the war. He also described why he disagreed with that decision. Upon graduating from Harvard in 1940, Jack's paper became a book entitled *Why England Slept*. With his father's

Lieutenant John F. Kennedy is shown in the PT-109 boat in the South Pacific, 1943.

financing and his own marketing efforts, Jack's book gained national recognition. It also gained him a voice in the international debate over foreign affairs.

SERVING THE NATION AT WAR

Although Kennedy began graduate school at Stanford in the fall, it was not long before he joined the

U.S. war effort. By October 1941, he had enlisted in the U.S. Navy and was working as an ensign in naval intelligence. On February 23, 1943, Kennedy began combat duty while stationed in the Pacific. There, he took command of the *PT-109* boat.

In August, a Japanese boat rammed Kennedy's boat. The *PT-109* was destroyed, and Kennedy's crew was scattered among the floating wreckage. Although he was injured, Kennedy saved the lives of three crew members. According to the Department of the Navy,

> *Kennedy was later awarded the Navy and Marine Corps Medal for his heroics in the rescue of the crew of PT-109, as well as the Purple Heart Medal for injuries sustained in the accident on the night of 1 August 1943.*[2]

Due to the injuries he sustained in the incident, Kennedy officially retired from the Navy in March

A Tragedy and Twist of Fate

After the *PT-109* was struck, Kennedy returned to the States to recover from his injuries. While visiting his family's Hyannis Port home in August 1944, the Kennedys received tragic news. Joe Jr., the eldest of the nine children, had been killed in duty. Joe Jr. had long been steered to a life of politics by their father, Joe Kennedy. With his oldest son gone, Joe turned his aspirations to Jack. Biographer Joyce Milton wrote, "A few weeks after Joe Jr.'s death, his father summoned Jack and informed him that it was his responsibility to fulfill the destiny that had been laid out for young Joe. He was to become the first Catholic president of the United States."[3]

*John F. Kennedy is shown campaigning for Congress
from Massachusetts' Eleventh District in 1946.*

1945. He was already well known as part of the
Kennedy family and now he was returning to civilian
life as a decorated war hero.

Serving the Nation at Home

Kennedy was considering a career in journalism
after being released from the Navy. However, the tragic

death of his older brother, Joe Jr., had redirected their father's plans. Joe Jr. had served in World War II as a pilot, but he was killed in 1944 when his plane exploded over the English coast. By September 1945, Jack was in Boston, Massachusetts, where he would run for U.S. Congress the following year. The young Kennedy took up residency in the state. Over the course of that year, he put together a campaign staff that included family members, locals, and war veterans who had served with him. Voters were invited to "teas" with his mother, Rose. Kennedy's father put plenty of money behind the campaign to ensure a win. Their combined efforts paid off, and at the age of 29, John F. Kennedy joined the 80th Congress on Capitol Hill in Washington, D.C.

Although young and somewhat inexperienced, Kennedy had a passion for politics and a strong interest in foreign policy. He was interested in defending democracy within the United States through discovering secret communists. Kennedy was also concerned about the international spread of communism.

Immediately following the conclusion of World War II, deep divisions set in between the world super powers: the United States and the Union of Soviet

Socialist Republics (USSR, or Soviet Union). This
political suspicion eventually came to be known as the
"Cold War." It was a power struggle between democracy
and communism. Democracy favored capitalism, which
supports privately owned businesses. Communism
favors a government-controlled society and publicly
owned property. During 1947, Kennedy planned on
making a trip to tour Europe with some other members
of Congress. The group wanted to learn more about
how communism appealed to laborers. Due to an
illness, Kennedy never made the complete trip. Despite
a number of absences due to health problems,
Kennedy was still able to accomplish enough in office
to appeal to voters, though. He was reelected to
Congress in 1948 and 1950.

Making Time for Family and Politics

In 1951, Kennedy met Jacqueline Bouvier at a
dinner party thrown by friends. The two met again in
May 1952 and began occasionally dating. Jack was in his
mid-thirties and was one of the most popular bachelors
in the country. However, he wanted to run for the
presidency some day. This meant showing the nation he
was a "family man." The couple's courtship survived the
pressures of Kennedy's U.S. Senate run in 1952. In

Senator John F. Kennedy and his bride, Jacqueline Lee Bouvier,
at their wedding in Newport, Rhode Island, September 12, 1953

September 1953, John F. Kennedy and Jacqueline
Bouvier married. Their youth, beauty, wealth, and
energy appealed to the nation. The Kennedy couple
was often in the news and admired by many people.

Kennedy's time in the Senate was not easy, though.
The issue of communism had deeply divided the

Jacqueline Bouvier

Jacqueline Bouvier Kennedy, known as "Jackie," was from a wealthy family with many social ties. She was a private person, was educated at Vassar, and had a strong interest in the arts. As her husband's popularity and political power grew, she stayed focused on protecting her family's privacy as well as maintaining a good image for Jack.

nation, and Wisconsin Republican Joe McCarthy had actively, and perhaps illegally, gone after supposed communists in government positions. The Kennedy family had personal ties to McCarthy. If the Senate were to censure McCarthy for his actions, it could hurt Jack's reputation and his chance at the presidency. In addition to this, Kennedy's health was not good, and he had to spend time in the hospital. Ultimately, because of his hospitalization, Kennedy was able to avoid taking a stand on the tactics McCarthy had used.

In November 1957, the Kennedy family grew with the birth of their daughter Caroline. Jack was also about to win a second term as a Senator. He had survived the McCarthy scandal, started a family, and grown in popularity among his peers and the voters. The time had finally come to run for the presidency.

John F. Kennedy holds his daughter, Caroline, while posing beside his wife,
Jacqueline Kennedy, at Hyannis Port, Massachusetts, in 1960.

Senator John F. Kennedy makes his way through a crowd of supporters.

THE CAMPAIGN AND
THE PRESIDENCY

John F. Kennedy wanted to be president and the plan to make it happen started well before his 1960 election. As a popular senator from Massachusetts, Kennedy was already preparing to win over the nation when he was reelected to the Senate in

1958. His father, Joe, funded Kennedy's senate reelection bid with an estimated $1.5 million. In fact, Kennedy even joked in earlier elections about the money spent by his family on campaigns. He would tell people that his father instructed him not to buy any more votes than necessary to win. By winning the Senate seat again, Kennedy was certain to remain in the public eye.

A Catholic President?

The most pressing question that seemed to face Kennedy's possible presidential nomination was not if he was qualified for the job, but rather, could a Catholic be elected president? Up to that point, there had never been a Catholic president. Many voters were concerned that if a Catholic were elected president, that person would follow the rules and teachings of the Roman Catholic Church instead of the voters' wishes. Kennedy had long known this would be a concern among voters. Early in his political career, he publicly

Why Religion Mattered

When Pilgrims first came to North America, they were seeking religious freedom. As the United States became a nation, the country's founding fathers held tightly to this belief of an individual's right to practice whatever religion he or she preferred. This separation of church and state has helped define the United States throughout its history. Most of the nation's founding fathers, however, were Protestant. Therefore, people of other faiths, such as Catholicism, have at times faced discrimination.

defended the right for a Catholic to serve in office by stating, "There is an old saying in Boston that we get our religion from Rome and our politics from home."[1]

Kennedy's campaign smartly focused on his youth, his beautiful family, his war heroism, and his successes as a Massachusetts congressman and senator. In 1958, Kennedy turned his focus on the presidency. His brother Bobby would serve as his campaign manager. John F. Kennedy looked at the issues facing the nation and began articulating a plan for a "New Frontier."

The Vice President's Popularity

Senator Lyndon B. Johnson was so popular in his home state of Texas that the voters there changed the laws to allow him to run for both vice president and senator at the same time. Usually, a person can only run for one office at a time. With this new law in place, Johnson was almost completely assured an office regardless of the outcome of the presidential election.

Once he became vice president, Johnson spoke out strongly on behalf of civil rights. He also gave direction to the moon-landing project and advocated for more scientific research in beating the Soviets in the "space race." This was the Cold War competition to be the first country to put a man in space and on the moon.

POLITICAL OPPONENTS

Before winning the presidency, Kennedy first had to win the Democratic Party nomination to run for the office. He faced more than one opponent. Senators Lyndon B. Johnson, Hubert Humphrey, and others also wanted the nomination. Johnson and Humphrey were very popular in their home and nearby states. Kennedy, however, prevailed on the convetion's first ballot. In order to help the campaign in the South, Kennedy asked Johnson to run as his vice president. Johnson accepted.

In a speech accepting his Democratic Party nomination, Kennedy called upon the nation to reignite its passion for democracy:

> I tell you the New Frontier is here ... Beyond that frontier are the uncharted areas of science and space, unsolved problems of peace and war, unconquered pockets of ignorance and prejudice, unanswered questions of poverty and surplus. It would be easier to shrink back from that frontier, to look to the safe mediocrity of the past, to be lulled by good intentions and high rhetoric—and those who prefer that course should not cast their votes for me, regardless of party. ... For the harsh facts of the matter are that we stand on this frontier at a turning-point in history. We must prove all over again whether this nation—or any nation so conceived—can long endure—whether our

Intending to Fight

"In the decade that lies ahead—in the challenging revolutionary sixties—the American Presidency will demand more than ringing manifestos issued from the rear of the battle. It will demand that the President place himself in the very thick of the fight, that he care passionately about the fate of the people he leads, that he be willing to serve them, at the risk of incurring their momentary displeasure."[2]

—John F. Kennedy

society—with its freedom of choice, its breadth of opportunity, its range of alternatives—can compete with the single-minded advance of the Communist system. … Can we carry through in an age where we will witness not only new breakthroughs in weapons of destruction—but also a race for mastery of the sky and the rain, the ocean and the tides, the far side of space and the inside of men's minds? …

That is the question of the New Frontier. That is the choice our nation must make—a choice that lies not merely between two men or two parties, but between the public interest and private comfort—between national greatness and national decline—between the fresh air of progress and the stale, dank atmosphere of "normalcy"—between determined dedication and creeping mediocrity.

All mankind waits upon our decision. A whole world looks to see what we will do. We cannot fail their trust, we cannot fail to try.[3]

Kennedy's powerful words were inspiring. But the young candidate still faced a battle to win the office. Kennedy would run against Richard Nixon, the two-term Republican vice president. Although it could be said that Nixon had more political experience,

Kennedy's youth and personality appealed to voters.
He looked good on camera and was relaxed in public.
Kennedy and Nixon were not that different in their
political agendas, though. Both were moderates in their
parties and had worked together in Congress earlier in
their careers. Their appearance, especially in the first-
ever televised debates, helped to shape the outcome of
the election.

A New President

The popular vote on Election Day split nearly in
half, but the electoral votes went to Kennedy by 302–
219. He was the youngest man ever elected president of
the United States, as well as the first Catholic to fill the
office. John F. Kennedy had fulfilled his father's
dream.

On January 20, 1961, a cold day in Washington,
D.C., America witnessed the inauguration of 43-year-
old Kennedy. He made it clear to the nation that he
would continue to fight for democracy, fight against
communism, and ultimately bring an end to the Cold
War by winning over the world:

> *Let every nation know, whether it wishes us well or ill, that*
> *we shall pay any price, bear any burden, meet any hardship,*

support any friend, oppose any foe to assure
the survival and the success of liberty.[4]

Kennedy would hold true to his word to fight for democracy, but he could not know the many challenges he would soon face as president.

A Growing Family

During the month of the presidential election, the Kennedy family added another member. John F. Kennedy Jr. was born on November 25, 1960.

U.S. President John F. Kennedy delivers his inaugural address after taking
the oath of office at the Capitol in Washington, D.C., on January 20, 1961.

Soviet Premier Nikita Khrushchev and U.S. President John F. Kennedy,
at the start of their historic talks, June 3, 1961

A Tumultuous
Three Years

President Kennedy's new role as the leader of the United States did not start with an easy task list. Kennedy was aware of the unrest at home made public by the civil rights movement. He was also aware of the growing friction between democratic nations and the communist leaders of the world. Since Kennedy first took a stand in the political tension between communism and democracy, the Cold War had only deepened. Relations between the United States and the Soviet Union were more tense than they had been at the end of World War II. By 1961, the superpowers were in an arms race and a political race to win over growing third-world countries. In addition, there was an escalating situation in Vietnam.

CREATING THE PEACE CORPS

One of the humanitarian measures President Kennedy put in place to slow communism was the Peace Corps. Founded in March 1961, the Peace Corps was established in part to show the world the national values of the United States. Kennedy was concerned that the Soviet Union was winning the world campaign among growing nations. With the Peace Corps program, he had an opportunity to introduce democracy to third-world nations that might otherwise be influenced to lean

Arms Race

The United States and the Soviet Union were in an arms race during the Cold War. Though a real war between the two nations was never fought during this time period, each country built more weapons, trained larger forces of troops, and increased its nuclear strength. This was meant to intimidate the other nation. It was an "arms race" to show military supremacy.

toward communism. The president especially wanted to leave this positive impression of democracy among the Latin American nations. He feared that Fidel Castro's influence was strong there, and he wanted to show the people that the United States offered hope for a brighter future. Political influence was not the only motivator behind starting the Peace Corps. Americans were also seeking ways to help others around the globe who may not have as many opportunities as Americans had been given. The idealistic nature of the program had groundings in the

The Cold War

During World War II, the United States and the Soviet Union had been allies. However, as the war came to an end, they had different ideas of what the postwar world should be like. Their conflicting ideas of capitalist democracy and communist states would drive them farther apart than they had ever been before World War II.

The Cold War spanned nearly half of the twentieth century, from the mid-1940s until 1990, when East and West Germany were finally united. The conflict was primarily between the United States and the Soviet Union, but each nation had its allies. These allies were usually neighboring countries, but the span was global. Many have described the division as a war between the two hemispheres of the world, Eastern and Western.

The Cold War was never a war in the true sense, with battlefields and direct fighting, but each superpower would support smaller, warring nations with arms, money, and sometimes their own troops. The Korean War, the Vietnam War, civil wars throughout the Middle East, and revolutionary uprisings in South and Central America all had ties to the Cold War or financial backing from it.

fact that the workers would truly be focused on
bettering the lives of the people they served. According
to the president's executive order, the volunteers were:

> *… expected to work and live alongside the nationals of the*
> *country in which they are stationed—doing the same work,*
> *eating the same food, talking the same language.*[1]

The Peace Corps were to serve as a grassroots effort
to further world development as well as curb the spread
of communism. This new program, however, was not
in place soon enough to stop events already happening
in Vietnam and Cuba.

COMMUNISM AND THE COLD WAR

Vietnam had not yet become a full-scale war and was
still low on the political radar of the United States.
The southern Asian nation was in a civil war between the
communist north and the anti-communist south.
Vietnam had been an area of conflict first during the
Korean War and again during the shaky peace treaty that
ended the Korean conflict. Upon this, France exited
the country and gave up its colonial hold on the nation.
President Kennedy feared that the unstable and
unprotected South Vietnam, led by president Ngo Dinh
Diem, would fall to its neighboring communist nations

The Discord in Vietnam during Kennedy's Presidency

In 1961, Kennedy sent advisors to Vietnam, where U.S. troops totaled 1,400. By 1968, the number of U.S. troops stationed in Vietnam would top 543,000. At the war's end, after ten years of U.S. involvement, more than 58,000 American troops would be missing or dead. Kennedy never predicted the war would last that long or claim that many lives. Ultimately, the decade of conflict in Vietnam would not prevent communist control of North Vietnam.

of North Vietnam, North Korea, and China. The new U.S. president sent a small number of troops and some top advisors to assess the situation in Vietnam. The advisors were to report back on possible aid needed from the United States.

The report from Vietnam instructed Kennedy to send more aid to Diem, including money and troops, with the hope of stabilizing the nation. Many of Kennedy's advisors recommended that he make the Vietnam aid a large-scale effort, including, if necessary, a declaration of war. Others did not want U.S. involvement and instead recommended Kennedy lead peace negotiations. Instead of either option, Kennedy sent a limited number of troops and refused to initiate a full-scale military buildup.

Castro and Cuba

The Cold War was not confined to the conflict in Vietnam. Cuba, an island to the south of the United States, had an increasingly friendly relationship with the

communist Soviet Union. Fidel Castro
had risen to power in Cuba shortly
before Kennedy was elected to the
U.S. presidency. Castro's motives,
with Soviet backing, quickly became
clear to the president. The Soviet
communist leaders wanted to gain a
stronghold and military base in the
Western Hemisphere. This had never
occurred in the history of the United
States.

Early in his presidency, Kennedy
decided that something had to be
done to quell the growing stronghold
communism had in Cuba. Only 90
miles (145 km) away from the United
States, Cuba was in a prime position
to hit U.S. land with nuclear weapons.
These suspicions and concerns for
national security led to the Bay of Pigs
Invasion in April 1961. The intention of this attack was
to overthrow the communist party and Castro. Cuban
exiles were supposed to invade the island nation and
take over the government, possibly assassinating Castro
if needed. The exiles were secretly trained by the

**The Berlin Wall:
A Symbol of
the Cold War**

Early in Kennedy's presi-
dency, he witnessed the
construction of the Berlin
Wall, which stood for
nearly 30 years. The
Berlin Wall finally came
down on November 9,
1989. President Ronald
Reagan was instrumental
in negotiating the wall's
destruction with Soviet
leader Mikhail Gorb-
achev. East Germany and
West Germany were
officially reunited as
Germany on October 3,
1990. Jubilant citizens
of the reunited nation
continued to tear down
the wall. Many people
kept chunks of the wall as
memorabilia. The wall's
destruction was one of
the major events marking
the end of the Cold War.

Fidel Castro (lower right) sits inside a tank during the
Bay of Pigs Invasion on April 17, 1961.

United States in Guatemala and armed with weapons.

To keep his new administration in good graces with
the public, Kennedy did not want any U.S. personnel
linked directly to the invasion. The attack was not well
planned, however, and the Cuban army quickly killed
or captured the invading troops. Surprisingly, the Bay
of Pigs Invasion did not shake the public's confidence in
Kennedy. "A Gallup poll reported that 83 percent of

Americans … had a favorable opinion of the president" after the failed invasion.[2] This invasion would not be Kennedy's last encounter with the Caribbean nation.

Nuclear Fears

The nuclear fallout of atomic bombs dropped on Japan during World War II was still on the public's mind in the early 1960s. The power, destruction, and long-term devastation caused by these nuclear weapons inspired both awe and fear.

The summer of 1961 brought more action in the Cold War— especially in West Berlin, which was located 200 miles (321.8 km) inside the communist sector of East Germany. That August, the government of East Germany began building a wall around three sectors of the city. The wall's purpose was to stop people from fleeing communist East Berlin for better jobs and lives in West Berlin. The wall divided families, kept people from jobs and loved ones, and physically divided the nation. In the month before the construction started, Kennedy addressed the people of Berlin via radio and television:

> The solemn vow each of us gave to West Berlin in time of
> peace will not be broken in time of danger. If we do not meet
> our commitments to Berlin, where will we later stand? If
> we are not true to our word there, all that we have achieved
> in collective security, which relies on these words, will mean

nothing. And if there is one path above all others to war, it is the path of weakness and disunity.[3]

While this address was moving, it did not stop the construction of the Berlin Wall.

Cuban Missile Crisis

During the autumn of 1962, Kennedy once again found himself at odds with Cuba. U.S. intelligence learned that the Soviet Union was equipping the small country with advanced weapons and fighter jets. In October, U.S. spy planes discovered that they were also constructing nuclear missile launch sites on the island. It was the outcome Kennedy and the U.S. public had feared since the failed Bay of Pigs Invasion: Cuba was nearing capability to launch nuclear war on the United States.

The resulting Cuban Missile Crisis threatened to become a nuclear confrontation between President Kennedy and the Soviet leader Nikita

Space Race

The United States and the Soviet Union were competing in outer space as well as on Earth. One of Kennedy's promises in office was to put a man on the moon. By flexing this scientific muscle, the United States hoped to show it had more advanced technology and therefore stronger military and social power. The Soviet Union hoped to show the same. Each nation wanted to be "the first in space" to prove to the rest of the world that it was the best. Outer space became yet another arena of competition in the Cold War.

Khrushchev. If construction continued in Cuba, the communists would have missiles in place that could hit almost any spot in the United States. Similarly, the United States had missile-launching sites in Turkey from which they could hit the Soviet Union. If the leaders could not reach an agreement, the nations faced the possibility of a nuclear war. The world held its breath.

After two weeks of tense negotiations, Kennedy called Khrushchev's bluff. The Soviets agreed to dismantle and remove the Cuban missile sites, and Kennedy secretly agreed to remove the U.S. missile bases from Turkey. The crisis was over, and the world breathed a sigh of relief. President Kennedy was seen as a hero for democracy. Supporters of communism did not necessarily agree.

BATTLES ON THE HOME FRONT

During the next year, Kennedy faced increasing pressure on the home front from civil rights leaders and activists, such as Dr. Martin Luther King Jr. and

The Bombings in Birmingham

On September 15, 1963, the Sixteenth Street Baptist Church in Birmingham, Alabama, was bombed. The bombers were people who claimed to be defending segregation and white supremacy. The church had served as the city's headquarters for the equal rights movement. The blasts killed four girls, ages 11 to 14: Addie Mae Collins, Denise McNair, Carole Robertson, and Cynthia Wesley.

Dr. Martin Luther King Jr.

Nobel Peace Prize winner Dr. Martin Luther King Jr. was killed by an assassin's bullet on April 4, 1968. After years of peaceful protest, King's life was taken in a violent act. During his life, King was a key player in the passing of the Civil Rights Act of 1964. He served as the voice of oppressed minorities throughout the nation and led the movement for equal rights.

Malcolm X. King and others were still fighting for racial equality in a nation that was very slowly desegregating its public school system. In the South, racial tensions were still extremely high from this cultural change. The movement was seeking similar equality in jobs and in general society. Demonstrations and arrests were happening nearly every month. Although Kennedy was attempting to move a civil rights bill through Congress, he was often met with fierce opposition from southern elected officials.

Kennedy continued fighting for equality. But the time was also coming to consider the 1964 presidential election. In his first term, President Kennedy had sent additional troops to Vietnam, stopped the dangerous Cuban Missile Crisis, and shown support for the civil rights movement.

Planning his 1963 trip to Texas to campaign for reelection began at the height of action in Kennedy's political career as well as the height of his popularity in the nation. No one knew what the fateful trip to Texas would hold for the young leader.

Ambassador Adlai Stevenson (center), U.S. delegate to the United Nations, meets
with Martin Luther King Jr. (left) in 1962. The meeting occurred as President John
F. Kennedy met with the American Negro Leadership Conference on Africa.

Vice President Lyndon B. Johnson meeting with President John F. Kennedy, 1963

THE TRIP TO DALLAS

fter his controversies, successes, and popularity of the previous three years, Kennedy seemed to be a "sure win" in the 1964 presidential election. However, the president was not going to take any chances. In November 1963, as a first

step in his campaign for reelection, Kennedy
realized that he needed to soothe tensions in the South
over his recent steps toward civil rights. Kennedy also
wanted to investigate the general political climate in
Texas. Vice President Lyndon B. Johnson was a Texan,
but this did not assure Kennedy a win in the state.
Instead, the Republican Party was gathering its forces
there to find candidates who might be a match to the
popular young president. In addition,
the Democratic Party in Texas was
feuding between two of its leaders,
Governor John B. Connolly and
Senator Ralph Yarborough.

Just one month prior to Kennedy's
arrival in Texas, an angry crowd had
struck Adlai Stevenson, the United
Nations ambassador, with a placard.
Vice President Johnson had also been
taunted. Kennedy was prepared for a
less-than-friendly reception, but he
seemed to have no concerns for his
personal safety.

Texas had a reputation at the time
for including both conservative
hotheads and a few communist

Travels of Previous Presidents

Prior to World War II,
presidents rarely traveled
across the nation or
internationally. After air
travel became a more
common method of
transportation, presidents
journeyed regularly by air.
In 1953, the president's
official airplane received
the unique call sign "Air
Force One." No other
airplane can use this call
sign. Every presidential
airplane since then has
been called Air Force
One.

extremists. Much of the world even viewed Texas as if it were still in the era of the Wild West. Still, Kennedy knew that to secure the election, he had to mend the break in his own political party before defeating the Republicans. He also had to reassure conservative southern voters that the movement toward civil rights was the best direction for the nation.

The Trip Agenda

The Texas trip included many people in Kennedy's administration. In addition to the first lady, the vice president and his wife, Lady Bird, were joining the

Johnson's Story

Lyndon B. Johnson's family had helped found Johnson City, Texas. Johnson was born in that area on August 27, 1908. In 1934, he married Claudia "Lady Bird" Taylor, and in 1937, he was elected to the House of Representatives. He continued to climb the political ladder, serving later in the Senate. After a few years, he served as the Minority leader and then as the powerful Majority leader. This success pushed Johnson toward a goal of reaching the presidency. But the popular Kennedy overpowered Johnson's shot at the 1960 election. When Johnson lost the presidential nomination, Kennedy offered him the vice presidency. Johnson accepted.

President Kennedy and Vice President Johnson did not always agree on the best approach toward world or national issues. Johnson's role in the vice presidential nomination, however, may have helped Kennedy win the 1960 election. With Johnson being a southerner, Kennedy's northern ties were balanced. Johnson would eventually win the 1964 presidential election by a landslide, earning 61 percent of the popular vote.

tour. Forty-two press members from Washington, D.C., and the surrounding area were also accompanying the president. More press from Texas would meet the party upon its arrival.

The group was to leave the Capitol on Thursday, November 21, and head to three cities. At each stop, the president would greet the public and speak with area politicians. In San Antonio, the president was to attend the dedication of the Aerospace Medical Health Center. In Houston, he was to speak to a citizens' organization for Latin Americans and speak on behalf of Congressman Albert Thomas at a dinner that evening. The first day would wrap up in Fort Worth, where the president would spend the evening.

The next morning, following an address to the Fort Worth Chamber of Commerce, everyone would fly to Dallas for a motorcade and lunch at

The Texas Feud

The political atmosphere in Texas that Kennedy wanted to assess had a lot to do with Senator Yarborough and Governor Connolly. Although both men were members of the Democratic Party, Yarborough was considered fairly liberal and Connolly was more conservative. If the president could not mend the rift between the two politicians, he knew it might hurt his chances of carrying Texas in the next election. He also wanted to calm the unrest among the extremists in the area. Some pockets in Texas believed Kennedy was secretly pro-communist. Meanwhile, there were communists in the state who resented the president for his actions against Cuba and the Soviet Union.

What Awaited Kennedy at the Trade Mart?

In addition to a steak lunch, the people of Texas also had gifts awaiting the president and first lady: a rocking chair and two Western saddles for Caroline and John Jr.

the Dallas Trade Mart. That was where the president would give a speech. After that, Kennedy would visit the LBJ ranch in Austin before departing for Washington, D.C. Dallas residents were so excited for the motorcade that the parade route map was published in the area paper for reference. Anyone wanting to get the best view of the motorcade could simply read the *Dallas Herald Times*.

John F. Kennedy and his wife, Jacqueline, arrive
at Dallas Love Field Airport on November 22, 1963.

The president and first lady were greeted by cheers from the crowd in Dallas.

THE PARADE AND
THE ASSASSINATION

The flight to Texas had been uneventful
for the president and his fellow travelers.
After making scheduled stops the previous day in San
Antonio, Houston, and Fort Worth, Air Force One
landed in Dallas on Friday, November 22.

It was just after 11:30 in the morning. Excited crowds met the presidential party at the airport, giving the first lady a bouquet of roses and cheering the president. The weather earlier in the morning had been overcast and rainy. Now, the clouds had broken and the day grew sunny.

THE FATEFUL MOTORCADE

With the bright skies and the surprisingly warm reception, the president and first lady entered the presidential limousine with Texas Governor John Connolly and his wife. The car also held two Secret Service agents. The motorcade had additional cars with Dallas police officers and the Dallas police chief, the vice president and his wife, and Senator Yarborough. Even more Secret Service agents rode in other cars. Following them were cars and buses filled with photographers, media, and members of both political parties. The motorcade's route was a ten-mile (16-km) stretch leading the

The Decision That May Have Changed History

The presidential limousine was shipped to Dallas, Texas, especially for the motorcade. In addition to having its top down, the vehicle could also be equipped with different tops. The car had a hard steel top, and a clear plastic "bubble" top. Although neither top was bulletproof at the time, either would have slowed the speed of a bullet and potentially made the gunshots nonfatal.

Due to poor weather the morning of November 22, 1963, the president had planned on using the bubble top. Upon arriving in Dallas to sunnier skies and warm temperatures, the president decided to use neither top.

group to the Trade Mart. That was where President Kennedy was to give a speech, accept some gifts, have lunch, and depart. As the vehicles made their way downtown, crowds lined the streets. People cheered and waved, holding signs and flags. Many had dressed their best to greet the president. Ladies inspired by the fashions of the first lady also wanted a glimpse of her in person.

At 12:30 p.m., after weaving through downtown on Main Street and then Houston Street, the motorcade made its turn by the Texas School Book Depository. The

---

The Speech That Was Never To Be

Kennedy never made it to the Trade Mart in Dallas on November 22, 1963. He was to have addressed a crowd of citizens who were beginning their lunches while the presidential motorcade approached the building. From Kennedy's remarks prepared for that lunch:

… I have spoken of strength largely in terms of the deterrence and resistance of aggression and attack. But, in today's world, freedom can be lost without a shot being fired, by ballots as well as bullets. The success of our leadership is dependent upon respect for our mission in the world as well as our missiles—on a clearer recognition of the virtues of freedom as well as the evils of tyranny. …

… A nation can be no stronger abroad than she is at home. Only an America which practices what it preaches about equal rights and social justice will be respected by those whose choice affects our future. Only an America which has fully educated its citizens is fully capable of tackling the complex problems and perceiving the hidden dangers of the world in which we live. And only an America which is growing and prospering economically can sustain the worldwide defenses of freedom, while demonstrating to all concerned the opportunities of our system and society. …[1]

president was now on Elm Street and moving toward a triple underpass that led to the freeway. Suddenly, a shot rang out, then a second and a third.

At first, people were unsure of what happened. Within seconds, it became clear that someone was firing shots at the motorcade. President Kennedy had been shot. He slumped over onto the first lady. Jackie struggled to the back of the car to grab a Secret Service agent for help. Quickly, the motorcade sped off to Parkland Memorial Hospital, which was just minutes away.

PANIC IN THE STREETS

No one knew where to turn. Some people were on the ground, covering their children. Others ran for shelter. Still others looked around, hoping to see the shooter. A few witnesses spotted a rifle being drawn back into a window of the Texas School Book Depository. The building was seven stories tall and served as a warehouse—the perfect place for a sniper.

False Arrests

In the chaos following the motorcade shootings, police wanted to quickly apprehend the shooter. This led to false arrests of people who were in the wrong place at the wrong time. Before Oswald was arrested in the Texas Theatre, a man was arrested after leaving an office building. He had been inside using the restroom while the shots were being fired. Upon exiting the building, he had no idea what just occurred in the motorcade. People nearby jumped the man and he was taken into custody for questioning.

Jacqueline Kennedy climbs on the back of the car to help a secret service agent into the vehicle after the president is shot in Dallas, Texas, November 22, 1963.

Hugh Aynesworth, who was with the *Dallas Morning News* at the time and was an eyewitness to the shooting, recalled,

> It was just complete chaos, because people didn't know where to run. Nobody knew where the shots were coming from. Nobody knew who'd been hit, if anybody. Nobody knew where to run to protect themselves.[2]

With people scattered in every direction, some of the

police and press followed the
motorcade to the hospital. Others
went into an immediate search for
the sniper. The location that seemed
most practical for a gunman was the
Texas School Book Depository.

The Hunt for an Assassin

At the time, journalists had to find
phones to call in the news. Moments
after the shooting, NBC reporter
Robert MacNeil was doing just that.
He had entered the Texas School
Book Depository to find a phone. On
his way into the building, he ran into
a man who was leaving. It later turned
out the man was the alleged shooter.

**The Texas School Book
Depository**

The seven-story building
known as the Texas
School Book Depository
provided a perfect view
of the presidential pa-
rade. The lethal shots
were fired from the sixth
floor, which was under
repair at the time. The
building had been rented
to numerous tenants,
including the book de-
pository company, and
saw a frequent turnover
of businesses, employ-
ees, and construction
workers during the time
of the assassination. The
site is now known as the
Dallas County Adminis-
tration Building.

Eyewitness accounts quickly led police to search the
building. Soon, MacNeil and other reporters found
themselves among swarms of officers. The reporters
and the officers did a sweep of the building, floor by
floor, for nearly the next hour. On the sixth floor, the
police found the sniper's nest. Three empty shell
casings were on the floor. After further searching, the
officers found the hidden rifle. The sniper, however,

was nowhere in the building.

Immediately following the shooting, many citizens joined the hunt for the sniper. There were not many immediate clues, but a gentleman by the name of Abraham Zapruder had a very important one. He had been filming the motorcade, and he was in possession of actual footage of the shooting.

Zapruder told the FBI about the film and where he thought the shots were fired from. Dallas Police wanted to see the film, too.

Officer J.D. Tippit

While questioning people immediately after the shootings, Dallas police officer J.D. Tippit was shot and killed. In the months following his murder, the local media received many donations for his family, who were left with no insurance. It is estimated that concerned citizens sent his widow and children more than $600,000.

Because of the limited technology, the film had to be developed before anyone could view the footage. While the film was developed, the hunt—and the violence—continued.

ANOTHER SHOOTING

Not even an hour after the shots were fired at the motorcade, another bulletin came across the Dallas Police Dispatch. Officer J.D. Tippit had been shot. A citizen who witnessed the shooting notified the police

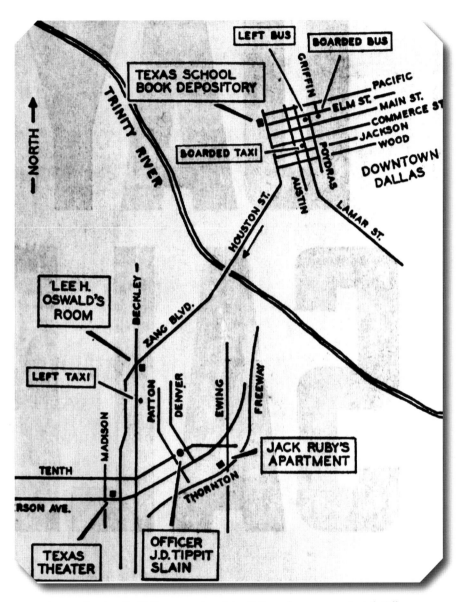

A map showing the Dallas area where John F. Kennedy was assassinated, Officer J.D. Tippit was killed, and Lee Harvey Oswald lived

Zapruder's Infamous Film

Abraham Zapruder captured one of the most historic pieces of film ever shot. He was witness to the presidential motorcade and filmed almost the entire sequence of the shooting. Within 48 hours of the shooting, *Life* magazine purchased all of the rights to the film. Zapruder told *Life* reporters that he was sickened by what he had filmed and he did not want them to exploit the homemade movie. *Life* respected Zapruder's wishes, and the scene in which the second bullet actually strikes Kennedy was not immediately shown to the public.

over Tippit's radio. The shooter was on the run, but this time the police were in pursuit.

At the Texas Theatre 30 minutes after the second shooting, police arrested the suspect in both shootings—his name was Lee Harvey Oswald.

*Lee Harvey Oswald at police headquarters in Dallas, Texas,
where he is held for questioning, November 22, 1963.*

Newspaper headlines about Kennedy's assassination

A Nation's Shock and Grief

While innocent citizens were being arrested and the police were still in pursuit of Oswald, everyone at Parkland Memorial Hospital moved in a state of urgency. The presidential motorcade had arrived there just minutes after the shooting. President Kennedy was quickly transferred to the emergency room, where doctors desperately attempted to save his life.

A team of neurosurgeons administered blood transfusions, heart massage, and other measures to the president. Members of the staff and media anxiously awaited news of his condition. The first lady sat in a state of shock, while Lady Bird Johnson attempted to comfort her.

Kennedy was not the only member of the party struck. Governor Connolly, who had been sitting in front of the president, was also critically wounded. Doctors were frantically working to save the governor. Despite multiple injuries, Connolly survived.

Soon, two priests arrived at the hospital. It became apparent to those waiting that Kennedy could not be revived. The priests were there to give the president his last rites.

At 1:00 p.m. on November 22, 1963, the doctors declared President Kennedy dead of a gunshot wound to the head.

REACTION TO THE NEWS

Malcolm Kilduff, the assistant White House press secretary, had the difficult job of officially announcing the president's death to the media. When he made the announcement approximately half an hour after the president died, the media were in shock. They quickly reacted, however.

Reporters dashed to phones throughout the hospital. Everyone needed to call in the breaking news. Television stations had "gone live" with special reports since hearing of the shooting only an hour before. On the CBS station, the first to address the nation with the announcement, news anchor Walter Cronkite became emotional. He choked up as he spoke to the nation:

From Dallas, Texas, the flash, apparently official: President Kennedy died at 1:00 p.m., Central Standard Time, 2 p.m.,

Continual Live Coverage

In the early 1960s, radios were still the main source of breaking news. Though television coverage did have the ability to do live broadcasts, the Kennedy assassination was the first time in history that nonstop, uninterrupted coverage was done for any major event. The first satellite technology was just being put in place and reporters still sent news to their stations from landline telephones. Cell phones did not exist, nor did the World Wide Web.

As coverage continued to stream in from Dallas, the nation watched. It is estimated that during the four days between Kennedy's shooting and his burial, over 90 percent of the televisions in the nation were turned to the live news. During the coverage, no commercials were ever run. The Museum of Broadcast Communications reported that the intense coverage cost the networks approximately $40 million—a huge sum in 1963.

*Eastern Standard Time—some 38 minutes
ago.[1]*

As news of President Kennedy's
shooting and death spread across the
nation, schools and businesses
everywhere closed their doors.
Children were sent home. People
stayed by their radios and television
sets, waiting for information and
grieving over the country's loss.
When the story first broke, the New
York Stock Exchange closed for the
day, with trading significantly down.
Americans were shocked. Their
young leader was gone.

"Where were you...?"
One of the phrases
mentioned by many who
were alive when President
Kennedy was killed is,
"Where were you when
you heard Kennedy was
shot?" The impact of the
news was so great that
most people recall exactly
where they were or what
they were doing when
they found out that the
president had been shot.

The Transition of Power

While the country swirled in shock and grief,
administration officials knew they had to secure the
presidency. Vice President Johnson had to be protected
and he would be sworn in as president on Air Force
One. Officials still did not know if the shots were fired
by a single assassin, or if the assassination was part of a
bigger plan to overthrow the government. With the

recent conflicts of the Cold War, anything was thought possible.

A little after 2:00 p.m., just half an hour after the public announcement of the president's death, the presidential party prepared to leave Parkland Memorial Hospital and return to the airport. The president's body had been placed in a bronze casket. Mrs. Kennedy, still covered in blood, refused to leave the casket as it was taken from the hospital.

By 2:30 p.m., Johnson, his wife, Mrs. Kennedy, and staff were aboard Air Force One at the Dallas airport. They were awaiting a judge to officially swear in Johnson as the president. Moments later, Federal Judge Sarah T. Hughes arrived. Using a Bible found in the president's sleeping quarters onboard, she swore in Johnson as the thirty-sixth president of the United States.

Charles Roberts from *Newsweek* was one of the reporters aboard Air Force One. He recalled the swearing in:

> Lady Bird stood on [Johnson's] right, and they faced the judge as she administered the oath. There was a minute or so of awkward silence and the president turned and kissed Lady Bird. He embraced Jackie, holding her by the elbows.

Lyndon B. Johnson is sworn in as president aboard Air Force One as Jacqueline Kennedy stands at his side.

> ... *There was a handshaking all around, but a very solemn sort of handshaking ... then the president turned and said, "Now, let's get airborne." That was eight minutes after he took the oath.* [2]

The swift series of events that day were remarkable to many of its witnesses. Sid Davis, who was at Dallas's Love Field Airport as the new president was departing, summarized the quick happenings well:

> It was the most amazing thing. What you had was the new president of the United States on the airplane, the body of the fallen president in a casket in the back of the airplane, the widow of the fallen president, and the wife of a new president on this plane going back to Washington after such a glorious day in politics for John F. Kennedy. As I watched [the plane] disappear ... it said something about the strength of this country, the fact that we had this thing happen, we didn't know who did it or why they did it, but the transition from one man to another was done in an orderly way. [3]

Davis's description of the event spoke of the strength and endurance of the shaken nation. In the days to come, the United States and the world would grieve together over the loss of the young leader. The search to bring the assassin to justice had already begun.

First Lady Jacqueline Kennedy, her dress stained with blood, stands with
Robert F. Kennedy, as her slain husband's casket is taken off the plane that
carried him from Texas at the end of the tragic day of November 22, 1963.

*Lee Harvey Oswald speaks with reporters the day after
John F. Kennedy's assassination.*

WHAT HAPPENED
TO OSWALD?

As the new president and the body of
the fallen president returned to
Washington, D.C., Dallas authorities held the alleged
assassin, Lee Harvey Oswald. Reporters gathered at the
city jail where Oswald was being held.

With Oswald in custody, officials searched for his family. Oswald's mother came forward to journalists, wishing to tell her side of the story. She was concerned for her financial well-being and wondered what people would think of her as the mother of an alleged assassin. Oswald's wife, Marina, was from Russia and spoke very little English. Reporters tried to gather more information from Oswald's mother and wife, but it proved fruitless. If Oswald was guilty, they did not seem to know of his plan.

Police continued to question Oswald, but he was calm under the pressure. He was interrogated for almost 12 hours over the next one and a half days. Assistant District Attorney Bill Alexander described Oswald as:

> *... almost arrogant and cocky. He answered almost every question with another question, and never gave that much information.* [1]

Presidential Assassinations

Four U.S. presidents have been assassinated while in office:
- ❖ Abraham Lincoln (1864)
- ❖ James A. Garfield (1881)
- ❖ William McKinley (1901)
- ❖ John F. Kennedy (1963)

Andrew Jackson, Franklin D. Roosevelt, Harry S. Truman, Gerald R. Ford (twice) and Ronald Reagan were shot at but not killed.

Two Days of Questioning

It would be two full days of questioning before Oswald would be transferred from the Dallas city jail to the county jail. In 1963, it was not a federal offense to kill the president. So, the state of Texas, rather than federal authorities, would be responsible for handling the alleged assassin. While the media hovered around the jailhouse, authorities continued to question the suspect. Oswald held his ground.

Who Was Lee Harvey Oswald?

Born in 1939, Lee Harvey Oswald was the third son of Marguerite and Robert Oswald, Sr. His father died shortly after his birth. By the time Lee was four years old, his mother had sent him and his brothers to an orphanage. Later, he was sent to a boarding school. Lee was reunited with his mother when he turned 12, but he continued to have behavior problems. He would often skip school and get in trouble with authorities.

In 1956, at the age of 17, Oswald joined the Marines and became a sharpshooter. Oswald still had discipline problems, and in 1959 he defected to Russia, where he wanted to become a citizen. Soon, the KGB (similar to the FBI) in Russia was tracking all of Oswald's movements.

Oswald married Marina Prusakova while living in Russia. In June 1962, Oswald returned to the United States with his bride and their first child.

Oswald was upset with the U.S. actions against Castro's Cuba. In the months leading up to Kennedy's assassination, Oswald went to Mexico City. While there, he attempted to get a Soviet visa. This would have let him travel to Cuba.

Jail Transfer

After almost two days in the Dallas city jail and numerous interrogations, authorities were growing concerned for Oswald's safety. It was decided that he would be transferred from the city jail to the county jail the next morning, November 24. The media reported news of the transfer, though the specific transfer time was not released.

The next morning, journalists, photographers, and camera crews continued to gather at the Dallas city jail. Everyone wanted to see the supposed assassin. Reporters were prepared for chaos. So were the police. They announced that they would transfer Oswald in an armored car. That car, however, did not fit into the secured basement loading area of the police station. In fact, another car was going to be used as the actual transfer car, with the armored car creating a diversion.

Shortly after 11:00 that morning, the suspect appeared in the basement corridor with police escorts at each side. A man in a dark suit suddenly stepped from the crowd and moved toward Oswald. A shot was fired. Oswald had been hit.

NBC reporter Tom Pettit was handling live coverage of the transfer and jumped on the action, yelling:

Who Was Jack Ruby?

Prior to killing Oswald, Dallas nightclub owner Jack Ruby had been around the Dallas scene for quite some time and was recognized by most police officers, fire fighters, and others in the emergency rescue field. Many people described him as a strange and isolated man. He was known for chasing action. Ruby always wanted to be where the media were. He had been present during the motorcade, was later seen at Parkland Memorial Hospital, and then at the Dallas city jail during the two days Oswald was held there. One of Ruby's club employees described his need for attention and action: "He really wanted to be somebody, but didn't have it in him. He hung around police headquarters. He was a nuisance around newspaper offices. He knew a tremendous number of people in Dallas, but he didn't have many friends."[3]

He's been shot! He's been shot! He's been shot! Lee Oswald has been shot! There's a man with a gun. There's absolute panic, absolute panic here in the basement of the Dallas police headquarters. Detectives have their guns drawn. Oswald has been shot. There's no question about it.[2]

The nation had just witnessed, on live TV, Dallas resident Jack Ruby shooting Lee Harvey Oswald.

Moments later, an ambulance was sent to retrieve Oswald. The gunshot wound to his lower abdomen looked severe. He was rushed to Parkland Memorial Hospital, where doctors attempted to save him. Authorities brought his wife and two children to the hospital. Meanwhile, police took Ruby into custody for the attempted murder and began questioning him. After two hours of emergency

The dramatic shooting of Lee Harvey Oswald, center, by Jack Ruby, right

surgery, doctors were unable to repair the damage from Oswald's gunshot wound. In the same emergency room of the same hospital where President Kennedy had died, Lee Harvey Oswald was pronounced dead 48 hours later. The president had been assassinated. Oswald, the alleged assassin, had been killed. And now Oswald's killer, Jack Ruby, was in custody. Confusion and conspiracy theories swept the nation. Had there been a larger plot to kill the president? ⟶

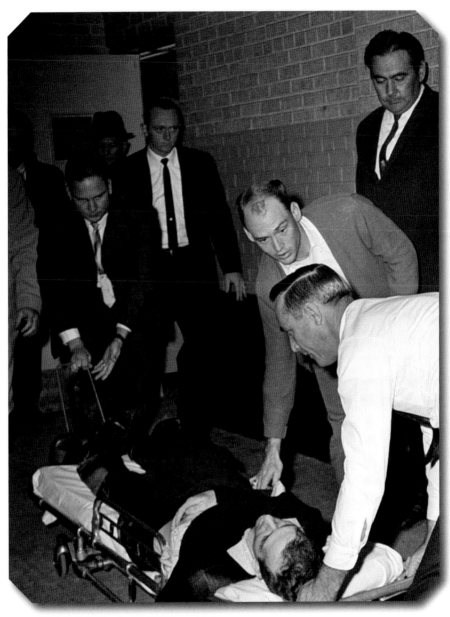

Lee Harvey Oswald is placed on a stretcher after being shot
in the stomach in Dallas, Texas, Sunday, November 24, 1963.

The flag-draped casket of slain President Kennedy lies in repose in the East Room of the White House.

THE FUNERAL

ate Friday evening on November 22, 1963, Air Force One returned to Washington, D.C. Security measures were very tight as the government made final funeral preparations for the slain president.

Mrs. Kennedy had not left her husband's body since departing from Parkland Memorial Hospital. She still wore the bloodstained suit and moved in a state of shock. While President Johnson secured the nation's safety, she planned President Kennedy's funeral. The body had been taken to Bethesda Naval Hospital for an autopsy and burial preparation. It was not until after 4:30 the following morning that the president's casket arrived at the White House. There, he would lie in repose, or privately, until being taken to Capitol Hill the following day, where he would lie in state.

As the casket was brought into the White House, Jackie Kennedy still remained by its side. White House press secretary Pierre Salinger witnessed the homecoming as the casket was moved to the East Room,

> *Mrs. Kennedy walked forward slowly and knelt by the casket in silent prayer. She then leaned forward and kissed the casket and slowly walked out of the door of the East Room.*[1]

The Search for Peace

"… peace does not rest in charters and covenants alone. It lies in the hearts and minds of all people. And if it is cast out there, then no act, no pact, no treaty, no organization can hope to preserve it without the support and the wholehearted commitment of all people. So let us not rest all our hopes on parchment and on paper; let us strive to build peace, a desire for peace, a willingness to work for peace, in the hearts and minds of all our people. I believe that we can. I believe the problems of human destiny are not beyond the reach of human beings."[2]

—*President John F. Kennedy*

Jacqueline Kennedy and daughter Caroline kneel beside the casket of John F. Kennedy in the rotunda of the Capitol in Washington, D.C., November 24, 1963.

She had not yet left her deceased husband, and only now, having seen him "home" for the final time, did she depart.

In the hours prior, people had flocked to the White

House. Even in the cold of the night, they waited outside the gate for the fallen president's body to return.

LYING IN STATE

The president would lie in repose at the White House for all of November 23. On November 24, his casket was taken to the Capitol for public viewing. As the nation continued to grieve, thousands of people arrived at the Capitol to pay their respects. It is estimated that nearly 250,000 people entered the Rotunda, and thousands more gathered outside. Roger Mudd of CBS News reported on the scene:

> ... without surcease, mourning Americans have moved through this Rotunda, first in two rows, single file on each side, at the rate of perhaps six thousand an hour; ... The line which formed here ... is estimated by police at five hundred thousand.[3]

The Parallels to President Lincoln

Jackie Kennedy wanted to honor her husband, the nation's president, in a manner similar to the way Abraham Lincoln was honored following his assassination. A book that detailed the burial of President Lincoln was consulted to aid in funeral planning.

Similarities between the two presidents often have been drawn, including their popularity among the public, their battles for civil rights, and their untimely deaths.

THE WORLD GRIEVES WITH THE UNITED STATES

On Monday morning, November 25, the processional began for President Kennedy's funeral and burial. The processional took the casket and mourners back to the White House and then on to St. Matthew's Cathedral, where a private funeral Mass was held. Numerous dignitaries and friends gave brief eulogies. When the Mass concluded, Jackie and her children stood on the steps waiting for the body of husband and father to pass by. As the pallbearers carried the casket to the caisson,

Oswald's Funeral

Having been shot and killed the day before, Lee Harvey Oswald was also buried on November 25, 1963. The only people to attend Oswald's funeral were his immediate family, including his mother, his brother Robert, and his wife, Marina, the press, and numerous authorities. Even the minister who had been hired to conduct the service did not arrive at the burial grounds. Later interviews with Oswald's family revealed that the brusque handling of the funeral procedures upset them. Authorities, however, were concerned for general security at the scene.

The entire event was a stark contrast from the tributes received by the president. The undertakers had Oswald's casket in a small building at the cemetery. When the time came to move the coffin to the plot, it became apparent that Oswald had no pallbearers. Instead, members of the media were pulled from the small crowd to carry the casket.

After a few short words and a prayer given by the officer who ran the cemetery, the crowd disbanded. Marina left her wedding band in the coffin. Later on, Oswald's grave marker was stolen.

three-year-old John Jr. raised his
hand and saluted his father.

The processional began the long,
somber walk to the Arlington National
Cemetery, where Kennedy would be
laid to rest. An eternal flame would
burn at his gravesite. Crowds lined the
entire course of the processional.
Dignitaries from every corner of the
world were in attendance—Russia,
England, France, the Philippines,
Canada, Ireland, India, Norway, West
Germany, Israel, and many others.

As the sun was setting, a 21-gun
salute was fired. Fifty jet planes flew
over the cemetery, and the Irish
Guard saluted the casket.

On Kennedy's gravesite
inscription, the words from his
inaugural address rang true:

> Let the word go forth
> From this time and place
> To friend and foe alike

An Eternal Flame

Colonel Clayton B. Lyle, a
Texas A&M graduate, was
the original designer of the
eternal flame at President
Kennedy's gravesite. Upon
Mrs. Kennedy's wish to
have an eternal flame as
part of her late husband's
memorial, the U.S. Army
Engineers went to work.
Led by Lyle, the team
created a temporary, yet
functional, design that was
in place in time for the
funeral. The design fed the
flame by a small propane
gas line. A natural gas line
now fuels the eternal flame
from underground.

In Paris, France, the Arc
de Triomphe honors the
Unknown Soldier with an
eternal flame. This was the
inspiration for Kennedy's
memorial.

A Horse Without a Rider

The caisson that carried President Kennedy's body was followed by Black-jack. The dark horse was saddled, but he carried no rider. In the ancient tradition honoring lost leaders and commanders, the horse was fitted with a saddle and reins. He also carried a sword and scabbard on his side, and in the stirrups were a pair of boots, placed backward. All of these things symbolized that a chief had fallen.

That the torch has been passed
To a new generation of Americans. ...
In the long history of the world
Only a few generations have been granted
The role of defending freedom
In the hour of maximum danger
I do not shrink from this responsibility
I welcome it ...[4]

The United States had just laid to rest its youngest leader, its first Catholic president, its inspiration for the space program, its champion against communism, and its hope for civil rights. As the nation mourned and regrouped, thousands would examine the events that led to such a tragedy.

Three-year-old John F. Kennedy Jr. salutes his father's casket on November 25, 1963. Jacqueline Kennedy, center, and daughter Caroline Kennedy are accompanied by Senator Edward Kennedy, left, and Attorney General Robert Kennedy.

Portrait of John F. Kennedy

THE CONSPIRACY THEORIES
AND A LEGACY

Who was John F. Kennedy? As president of the United States, he led the nation through 1,000 tumultuous days in office. As a celebrity in the eyes of many, he was a vibrant person, full of charm, grace, humor, wit, and intelligence. He was wealthy, good looking, and energetic—very appealing as a person and president.

John F. Kennedy was part of a prominent New England family that had accomplished the American dream. In the span of just three generations, the Kennedy family went from average Irish immigrants to successful and wealthy business people who influenced both society and politics.

It was Kennedy's destiny to continue this leadership and to uphold the family's name and place in society. Tragically, it was also his fate to be assassinated at the height of his popularity and success. His assassination left many to ask: Why would someone want to kill the president?

SEARCHING FOR A MOTIVE

Soon after the assassination, U.S. Chief Justice Earl Warren was appointed by President Johnson to head a bipartisan commission to investigate the details surrounding Kennedy's death. The investigation involved reenactments of the crime scene and detailed forensic testing of the bullets and the alleged weapon. Investigators also checked Oswald's background and military involvement, and even the background of Jack Ruby, Oswald's assassin. The Commission interviewed

Oswald's family and witnesses to the shootings. After a lengthy investigation, the Warren Commission found Oswald guilty as the assassin. From the study's conclusion:

> *The shots which killed President Kennedy and wounded Governor Connally [sic] were fired by Lee Harvey Oswald. This conclusion is based upon the following:*
>
> *(a) The Mannlicher-Carcano 6.5-millimeter Italian rifle from which the shots were fired was owned by and in the possession of Oswald.*
>
> *(b) Oswald carried this rifle into the Depository Building on the morning of November 22, 1963.*
>
> *(c) Oswald, at the time of the assassination, was present at the window from which the shots were fired.*
>
> *(d) Shortly after the assassination, the Mannlicher-Carcano rifle belonging to Oswald was found partially hidden between some cartons on the sixth floor and the improvised paper bag in which Oswald brought the rifle to the Depository was found close by the window from which the shots were fired.*

PHOTOGRAPH FROM ZAPRUDER FILM

PHOTOGRAPH FROM RE-ENACTMENT

PHOTOGRAPH THROUGH RIFLE SCOPE

DISTANCE TO STATION C	181.9 FT.
DISTANCE TO RIFLE IN WINDOW	218.0 FT.
ANGLE TO RIFLE IN WINDOW	18°03′
DISTANCE TO OVERPASS	307.1 FT.
ANGLE TO OVERPASS	+0°44′

FRAME 255

*Exhibit 901 from the Warren Commission Report
of the assassination of President John F. Kennedy*

(e) *Based on testimony of the experts and their analysis of
films of the assassination, the Commission has
concluded that a rifleman of Lee Harvey Oswald's
capabilities could have fired the shots from the rifle used
in the assassination within the elapsed time of the
shooting. The Commission has concluded further that*

> Oswald possessed the capability with a rifle which
> enabled him to commit the assassination. …
>
> (f) Oswald lied to the police after his arrest concerning
> important substantive matters.
>
> (g) Oswald had attempted to kill Maj. Gen. Edwin A.
> Walker (Retired, U.S. Army) on April 10, 1963,
> thereby demonstrating his disposition to take human
> life.[1]

In addition to finding Lee Harvey Oswald guilty, the
Warren Commission's report also ultimately showed
that he had acted alone:

> The Commission has found no evidence that either Lee
> Harvey Oswald or Jack Ruby was part of any conspiracy,
> domestic or foreign, to assassinate President Kennedy.[2]

But some facts surrounding the case were concealed, or
classified, for many years.

THE DEBATE OVER THE WARREN COMMISSION REPORT

Although the committee that assembled the Warren
Commission Report used a number of outside experts

*The Warren commission meets for the first time on December 5, 1963. The group,
from left, includes: Allen W. Dulles, Hale Boggs (D-LA.),
John Sherman Cooper (R-KY), Chief Justice Earl Warren,
Richard Russell (D-GA), John J. McCloy, and Gerald R. Ford (R-MI).*

and examined numerous testimonies, its findings
remain unacceptable to conspiracy theorists. Author
and attorney Gerald Posner concludes,

> *A network of amateur sleuths was prepared to check [the
> report's] accuracy against the research they had compiled
> since the day of the murder. An eclectic mixture of people
> across the country, many of whom were admitted leftists
> and were suspicious that a Communist was blamed for the
> murder in a right–wing city, had independently begun
> collecting everything printed on the subject.*[3]

CONSPIRACY THEORIES

President Kennedy had many loyal followers. These people were looking for a more convincing explanation for his death than a single act of violence.

Although a full investigation and trials occurred after Kennedy's assassination, so did a number of conspiracy theories. Over the years, hundreds of books and Web sites have been published in attempts to explain these possible conjectures. In the 1960s, people were still very sensitive to the number of conflicts that surrounded the presidency. These included the Bay of

---

Another Lost Leader

For many years, Robert Kennedy served as a campaign adviser to his older brother. He supported the civil rights movement and was a strong liberal voice in the Senate from 1965 to 1968. On June 5, 1968, assassin Sirhan Sirhan shot Robert Kennedy. Kennedy died the next day. He had just won the Democratic primary in California.

A mere two months before, Kennedy had spoken in Indianapolis and had to announce the assassination of Martin Luther King, Jr.:

We can do well in this country. We will have difficult times; we've had difficult times in the past; we will have difficult times in the future. It is not the end of violence; it is not the end of lawlessness; it is not the end of disorder.

But the vast majority of white people and the vast majority of black people in this country want to live together, want to improve the quality of our life, and want justice for all human beings who abide in our land.

Let us dedicate ourselves to what the Greeks wrote so many years ago: to tame the savageness of man and make gentle the life of this world.[4]

He could not have known that he would suffer the same tragic fate so soon after his request for peace.

Pigs Invasion, the standoff over the Cuban Missile
Crisis, and the growing conflict in Vietnam. Many
people were also suspicious of opponents to the civil
rights movement, which Kennedy had supported.

One of the conspiracy theories proposed that the
Central Intelligence Agency (CIA) acted with the Mafia
to have Kennedy assassinated. Another alleged that
Oswald had ties with the Russian KGB, and the
motivation for the crime was to punish Kennedy for his
actions against Cuba and Communism. Still another
theory held that white supremacists were acting out
against Kennedy's support for equality and his push to
pass the Civil Rights Act. Some people even suspected
the vice president or held the city of Dallas responsible.
One of the most popular conspiracy theories was even
made into a movie, *JFK*, which won two academy awards
despite widespread criticism for historical inaccuracies.

None of these conspiracies have been proven,
however, and the Warren Commission's report still
stands as the final answer on the events leading to
President Kennedy's assassination.

REOPENING THE CASE

In 1976, the House Select Committee on
Assassinations was established to reopen the Kennedy

Camelot

The idyllic world of Camelot was portrayed in the 1960s musical by the same name. After her husband's assassination, Jackie revealed that the music from the show had been a family favorite. The "brief, shining moment" of the fictional Camelot became a social parallel and description of the young, heroic John F. Kennedy's time in the White House.

assassination case. Many people had felt the Warren Commission did not fully succeed in its investigations. Although citing Lee Harvey Oswald as the gunman, the Select Committee also concluded, based on an audio tape that was later completely discredited, that President Kennedy's assassination was probably the "result of a conspiracy."[5] The committee also investigated the murder of Dr. Martin Luther King Jr.

Protecting a Fallen Hero

In addition to honoring him in life, Jackie also wanted to ensure that her husband would be remembered well in death. After planning the funeral and burial at Arlington National Cemetery, she turned to building a presidential library and legacy. Jackie oversaw the architecture of the John F. Kennedy Presidential Library and Museum in Boston, Massachusetts. The museum was dedicated in 1979. It serves as a library that holds the majority of the president's papers and records. The library also honors Kennedy and acts as a cultural and educational center.

The John F. Kennedy Presidential Library and Museum in Boston, Massachusetts

Both Jackie and Robert Kennedy vigorously protected Jack's memory and reputation in the years following the shooting. The era of his presidency eventually became known as "Camelot." By carefully following what was published and what was displayed in the media, Jackie and Robert were able to protect this ideal, which was long held by the grieving nation.

The Legacy of JFK

Kennedy's life and the dramatic events surrounding his death have long been fixed in the world's mind. Whatever mistakes he may have made during his time as president and in his private life have become part of the mystery that still surrounds the Kennedy family. It will never be known what he might have accomplished had his life not been cut short. However brief his time in office, John F. Kennedy inspired a younger generation, helped reenergize a nation, and left a legacy that will not soon be forgotten. Kennedy asked Americans and the people of the world to strive for a greater good, as articulated in his inaugural address on January 20, 1961:

> *My fellow Americans: ask not what your country can do for you—ask what you can do for your country. My fellow citizens of the world: ask not what America will do for you, but what together we can do for the freedom of man.* [6]

President Kennedy and his son, John Jr., stand hand-in-hand at the White House.

TIMELINE

1917

John Fitzgerald Kennedy is born on May 29 in Brookline, Massachusetts.

1939

Lee Harvey Oswald is born on October 18 in New Orleans, Louisiana.

1940

Kennedy graduates from Harvard University in June.

1946

Kennedy is elected to Congress in Massachusetts in November and is reelected in 1948 and 1950.

1952

Kennedy is elected to the U.S. Senate in November.

1953

Kennedy marries Jacqueline Bouvier on September 12.

1940

1941

1943

Kennedy's book, *Why England Slept,* is published in July.

Kennedy begins serving in World War II in October as an Ensign in the U.S. Navy.

The Japanese destroyer *Amagiri* strikes Kennedy's *PT-109* boat on August 3. Despite his injuries, Kennedy helps save the crew.

1957

1958

1960

Daughter Caroline Bouvier Kennedy is born on November 27.

Kennedy is reelected in Massachusetts to the U.S. Senate.

Kennedy wins the U.S. presidential election in November.

TIMELINE

1960	1961	1961

John F. Kennedy Jr. is born on November 25.	Kennedy is inaugurated as president on January 20.	The Bay of Pigs Invasion is launched on April 17.

1962	1963	1963	1963

The Cuban Missile Crisis between the United States and the Soviet Union occurs between October 22–28.	Lee Harvey Oswald purchases a firearm in January under the alias A.J. Hidell.	Kennedy leaves Washington, D.C., on November 21 for Texas.	Kennedy is struck at 12:30 p.m. by shots from alleged assassin Lee Harvey Oswald in Dallas, Texas, on November 22.

1961

1961

1962

Lee Harvey Oswald
marries Marina
Prusakova on April 30
in Russia.

In Germany, the first
section of the Berlin
wall is erected in
August. The wall
symbolizes the struggle
between communism
and democracy.

American Lieutenant
Colonel John H. Glenn
Jr. successfully orbits
Earth.

1963

1963

1963

1963

Kennedy is
pronounced dead
at 1:00 p.m. on
November 22.

Suspect Lee
Harvey Oswald is
shot at 11:21 a.m.,
November 24,
during his jail
transfer.

Lee Harvey
Oswald is
pronounced dead
at 1:25 p.m.,
November 24.

Kennedy is laid to
rest at Arlington
National Cemetery
on November 25.
Lee Harvey
Oswald is also
buried this day in
Texas.

Essential Facts

Date of Event
November 22, 1963

Place of Event
Dallas, Texas

Key Players
- ❖ Lyndon B. Johnson
- ❖ John F. Kennedy
- ❖ Jacqueline Kennedy
- ❖ Lee Harvey Oswald
- ❖ Jack Ruby
- ❖ U.S. Chief Justice Earl Warren
- ❖ Abraham Zapruder

Highlights of Event
- ❖ In November 1960, John F. Kennedy was elected president of the United States.
- ❖ The Bay of Pigs Invasion occurred on April 17, 1961. Lee Harvey Oswald was angered by U.S. action against Cuba.
- ❖ Between October 22 and 28, 1962, the Cuban Missile Crisis occurred between the United States and the Soviet Union. Kennedy and Russian leaders compromised and avoided nuclear war.

❖ Lee Harvey Oswald purchased a firearm under the alias A.J. Hidell in January 1963.

❖ On November 22, 1963, John F. Kennedy was shot by alleged assassin Lee Harvey Oswald. Kennedy was taken to Parkland Memorial Hospital and pronounced dead.

❖ Abraham Zapruder filmed almost the entire sequence of the assassination.

❖ Suspect Lee Harvey Oswald was shot during his jail transfer in Dallas, Texas, by Jack Ruby on November 24, 1963. Oswald was taken to Parkland Memorial Hospital and pronounced dead.

❖ On November 25, 1963, Kennedy was laid to rest at Arlington National Cemetery. Lee Harvey Oswald was buried in Texas.

❖ The Warren Commission found Oswald guilty as the assassination of John F. Kennedy.

Quote

"[...] peace does not rest in charters and covenants alone. It lies in the hearts and minds of all people. And if it is cast out there, then no act, no pact, no treaty, no organization can hope to preserve it without the support and the wholehearted commitment of all people. So let us not rest all our hopes on parchment and on paper; let us strive to build peace, a desire for peace, a willingness to work for peace, in the hearts and minds of all our people. I believe that we can. I believe the problems of human destiny are not beyond the reach of human beings."

—*John F. Kennedy*

ADDITIONAL RESOURCES

SELECT BIBLIOGRAPHY

Posner, Gerald. *Case Closed: Lee Harvey Oswald and the Assassination of JFK*. New York: Random House, 1993.

Schlesinger Jr., Arthur. *A Thousand Days: John F. Kennedy in the White House*. 1965. Ed. David Sobel. Abr. Ed. New York: Black Dog & Leventhal, 2005.

Semple Jr., Robert B. *Four Days in November*. New York: St. Martin's, 2003.

The President John F. Kennedy Assassination Records Collection. The National Archives. <http://www.archives.gov/research/jfk/>.

Trost, Cathy, The Newseum, Susan Bennett. *President Kennedy Has Been Shot*. Naperville, IL: Sourcebooks, 2003.

FURTHER READING

Anderson, Catherine Corley. *John F. Kennedy*. Presidential Leaders series. Minneapolis: Lerner, 2004.

Gogerly, Liz. *The Kennedy Assassination: 22nd November 1963*. Days That Shook the World series. Austin, TX: Raintree Steck-Vaughn, 2003.

Spencer, Lauren. *The Assassination of John F. Kennedy*. Library of Political Assassinations series. New York: Rosen Pub. Group, 2002.

The Assassination of John F. Kennedy. Ed. Carolyn McAuliffe. At Issue in History series. San Diego, CA: Greenhaven Press, 2003.

Web Links

To learn more about the assassination of John F. Kennedy, visit ABDO Publishing Company on the World Wide Web at **www.abdopublishing.com.** Web sites about the assassination of John F. Kennedy are featured on our Book Links page. These links are routinely monitored and updated to provide the most current information available.

Places to Visit

John F. Kennedy Presidential Library and Museum
Columbia Point, Boston, MA 02125
866-JFK-1960, 617-514-1600
www.jfklibrary.org
The John F. Kennedy Presidential Library and Museum holds the majority of the president's papers and records. It also serves as a shrine to the late president and acts as a cultural and educational center.

Arlington National Cemetery
Arlington, VA 22211
www.arlingtoncemetery.org
This military cemetery is the gravesite of John F. Kennedy. Kennedy's grave is marked with an eternal flame, which was lit by Mrs. Kennedy during the funeral.

The Sixth Floor Museum at Dealey Plaza (Texas School Book Depository)
411 Elm Street, Dallas, TX 75202
214-747-6660
www.jfk.org
This museum is located in the building that the Texas School Book Depository Company leased at the time of Kennedy's assassination. The sixth floor is the site of the sniper's nest, and is now a museum dedicated to the life and assassination of John F. Kennedy.

GLOSSARY

agenda
An underlying idea, plan, or program, often used in politics.

alias
An assumed name, personality, or identity.

alleged
Accused but not proven; something assumed to be true.

apprehend
To arrest or seize someone, usually an act of capture.

assassin
A person who commits a murder, usually with a political motive.

caisson
A carriage that carries the body of a deceased president during a presidential funeral.

communism
A political theory that supports state-wide ownership of all property and no private property.

eternal
To go on or exist forever.

FBI
Abbreviation for the Federal Bureau of Investigation. An agency of the U.S. government that deals with security and counter-intelligence.

KGB
The former Soviet Union's equivalent of the FBI.

lie in repose
The period of time during which a deceased official's body is available for private mourning.

lie in state
>The period of time during which a deceased official's body is available for public mourning.

motorcade
>A procession of motor vehicles; the official group of vehicles that carries the president and his colleagues.

nomination
>The state of being appointed to an office or to be proposed as a candidate for an office.

nuclear
>Used in or produced by a nuclear reaction, which causes destructive power.

segregation
>The enforced separation of a group by race, class, or ethnicity.

sniper
>Someone who shoots at an exposed person or persons, usually from a concealed area.

transfusion
>An injection of blood from one person into another person.

white supremacy
>A set of beliefs held by groups that think the white race is superior over other races and that nonwhite groups should be subordinated.

Source Notes

Chapter 1. Buying a Gun

1. Gerald Posner. *Case Closed: Lee Harvey Oswald and the Assassination of JFK*. New York: Random House, 1993. 107.

Chapter 2. The Kennedy History

1. Joyce Milton. *John F. Kennedy*. New York: Biography-DK Publishing, 2003. 17.

2. Department of the Navy: Naval Historical Center. June 18, 2002. 28 Jan. 2007 <http://www.history.navy.mil/faqs/faq60-2.htm>.

3. Joyce Milton. *John F. Kennedy*. New York: Biography-DK Publishing, 2003. 71.

Chapter 3. The Campaign and the Presidency

1. Robert Dallek. *An Unfinished Life: John F. Kennedy, 1917–1963*. New York: Little, Brown, 2003. 146.

2. John F. Kennedy. "The Presidency in 1960." National Press Club, Washington, D.C. 14 Jan. 1960. <http://www.jfklibrary. org/Historical+Resources/Archives/Reference+Desk/Speeches/ JFK/JFK+Pre-Pres/The+Presidency+in+1960.htm>.

3. John F. Kennedy. Address of Senator John F. Kennedy Accepting the Democratic Party Nomination for the Presidency of the United States. Memorial Coliseum, Los Angeles. 15 July. 1960. <http://www.jfklibrary.org/Historical+Resources/Archives/ Reference+Desk/Speeches/JFK/JFK+PrePres/Address+of+ Senator+John+F.+Kennedy+Accepting+the+Democratic+Party+ Nomination+for+the+Presidency+of+t.htm>.

4. John F. Kennedy. Inaugural Address. United States Capitol, Washington, D.C. 20 Jan. 1961. John F. Kennedy Presidential Library & Museum, Boston, MA.

Chapter 4. A Tumultuous Three Years

1. Robert Dallek. *An Unfinished Life: John F. Kennedy, 1917–1963*. New York: Little, Brown, 2003. 339.

2. Joyce Milton. *John F. Kennedy*. New York: Biography-DK Publishing, 2003. 118.

3. John F. Kennedy. Radio and Television Report to the American People on the Berlin Crisis. The White House, Washington D.C. 25 July. 1961. <http://www.jfklibrary.org/ Historical+Resources/Archives/Reference+Desk/Speeches/JFK/ 003POF03BerlinCrisis07251961.htm>.

Chapter 5. The Trip to Dallas

None.

Chapter 6. The Parade and the Assassination

1. John F. Kennedy. "Remarks Prepared for Delivery at the Trade Mart in Dallas." 22 Nov. 1963. 17 Jan. 2007 <http://www. jfklibrary.org/Historical+Resources/Archives/Reference+Desk/ Speeches/JFK/003POF03TradeMart11221963.htm>.

2. Cathy Trost, The Newseum, and Susan Bennett. *President Kennedy Has Been Shot*. Naperville, IL: Sourcebooks, 2003. 28.

Chapter 7. A Nation's Shock and Grief

1. Walter Cronkite. CBS Special Bulletin. CBS News Archives. 22 Nov. 1963.

2. Cathy Trost, The Newseum, and Susan Bennett. *President Kennedy Has Been Shot*. Naperville, IL: Sourcebooks, 2003. 120.

3. Ibid. 121.

Chapter 8. What Happened to Oswald?

1. Gerald Posner. *Case Closed: Lee Harvey Oswald and the Assassination of JFK*. New York: Random House, 1993. 345.

2. Tom Pettit. NBC Live Broadcast. NBC News Archives. 24 Nov. 1963.

3. Gerald Posner. *Case Closed: Lee Harvey Oswald and the Assassination of JFK*. New York: Random House, 1993. 356.

Chapter 9. The Funeral

1. Cathy Trost, The Newseum, and Susan Bennett. *President Kennedy Has Been Shot*. Naperville, IL: Sourcebooks, 2003. 173.

2. John F. Kennedy. Address Before the 18th General Assembly of the United Nations. New York. 20 Sept. 1963. <http://www.jfklibrary.org/Historical+Resources/Archives/Reference+Desk/Speeches/JFK/003POF03_18thGeneralAssembly09201963.htm>.

3. Roger Mudd. CBS News Archives. 24 Nov. 1963.

4. "John Fitzgerald Kennedy." Arlington National Cemetery Website. 27 Mar. 2006. 6 June 2007 <http://www.arlingtoncemetery.net/jfk.htm>.

Chapter 10. The Conspiracy Theories and a Legacy

1. Report of the President's Commission on the Assassination of President Kennedy. *Web version based on Report of the President's Commission on the Assassination of President John F. Kennedy,* Washington, D.C.: United States Government Printing Office, 1964. 1 volume, 888 pages. <http://www.archives.gov/research/jfk/warren-commission-report/chapter-1.html>.

2. Ibid.

3. Gerald Posner. *Case Closed: Lee Harvey Oswald and the Assassination of JFK*. New York: Random House, 1993. 412.

4. Robert F. Kennedy. Statement on the Assassination of Martin Luther King. Indianapolis, IN. 4 Apr. 1968. <http://www. jfklibrary.org/Historical+Resources/Archives/Reference+Desk/Sp eeches/RFK/Statement+on+the+Assassination+of+Martin+Luther +King.htm>.

5. "Report of the Select Committee on Assassinations of the U.S. House of Representatives." *Web version based on the Report of the Select Committee on Assassinations of the U.S. House of Representatives.* Washington, D.C.: United States Government Printing Office, 1979. 1 volume, 686 pages. 22 May 2007 <http:// www.archives.gov/research/jfk/select-committee-report/>.

6. John F. Kennedy. Inaugural Address. United States Capitol, Washington, D.C. 20 Jan. 1961.

INDEX

ABOUT THE AUTHOR

Patricia M. Stockland has written more than 20 books for children and young adults, as well as numerous poems, scholarly articles, and marketing pieces. Her writing has won national and regional awards, including a Selector's Choice as the 2006–2007 NSTA-CBC's Outstanding Science Trade Book for K-12, the Association for Educational Publishing's Distinguished Achievement Award, the AEP's nomination for a Golden Lamp Award, and a nomination as a MAGS scholar. She has been an editor and author for the past ten years and holds an M.A. in Literature and a B.A. in English. Patricia lives and works in Minnesota.

PHOTO CREDITS